A HUNGER
CALLED MUSIC

a verse history of black music
Meredith Nnoka

Winter Soup Bowl Chapbook
2016 Selection 2 of 2   CB2

Cover Art and Interior Design by Victoria Dinning

Copyright ©2016 by Meredith Nnoka

ISBN: 978-1-936196-78-4

C&R Press
Conscious & Responsible
www.crpress.org

For special discounted bulk purchases please contact:
C&R Press sales@crpress.org

TABLE OF CONTENTS

ACKNOWLEDGEMENTS

All definitions were taken from the *Oxford English Dictionary*. I would like to thank Ellen Doré Watson and Kevin Quashie for their unwavering support, as well as my friends and family for theirs. I would also like to thank the people whose stories I have borrowed, both the real stories and the invented ones. I can only hope that their voices were treated with the dignity and individual attention they deserve.

Poems from this collection originally appeared in Massachusetts *Review. Mandala Journal, Riding Light, HEArt Online*, and *The Ghazal Page*.

FIELD HOLLER

noun

A melodic call with abrupt swooping changes of pitch, which originated among slaves on Southern plantations as a type of work song and is freq. viewed as a predecessor to blues music.

WORKSONG

After Yusef Komunyakaa

My worksong is about the heart
and figuring out how to mend it—
it can only belong with your
wrought and tender voice.

Your worksong is the puzzle
of a body, how wind rustles
a ribcage, how light permeates
the skin without hitting bone.

Our worksong is a wine glass
splintering before it breaks,
the sound a mouth makes
when the spirit climbs out.

This worksong is the careful
alchemy of music becoming
marrow—a story hidden in
the heartline, in the blood.

CHAIN-GANG GHAZAL

one man falls. *oh long john, we sing, he long gone*. then
a crack, and he's up like lazarus rising from his back.

in the alabama august, we stand out along the railroad,
hammering till we feel the muscles crying in our backs.

the white men come with rifles, they walk behind us, they
scan the woods and say they'll have us lying on our backs.

we're all lonely voices quivering through the airless heat;
we don't pray, but we know god's been eyeing our backs.

we begin at dawn, sweat already spilling down our necks—
a hundred of us chained together, frying our backs.

we are men first, fathers second, husbands third, & inmates
last. we'll be working till we're out here dying on our backs.

BOLL

After Essex Hemphill

in the cotton fields
i pick the bolls
till i bleed.
no white man
on a horse,
no shotgun held
against his chest
will stop
this stigmata—
too many hands
with similar wounds
to linger on one.
he doesn't know
how deep
this bleeding goes—
one day, maybe
straight through.
in the cotton fields
i pick the bolls
till i bleed.
long may this song
be sung.

TWENTY-TWO SINGS

Out early on the railroad, Twenty-Two
and his men would sing to raise their souls up
from the dirt, hammers keeping time against
the tracks, the sun beating down on their backs.

Over the hollering in his bones. he
would bring his hammer down until his palms
bled, would sing from the good book until he
ran out of verses, until his voice shook.

How many years in the chains did it take
before Twenty-Two understood he would
never walk free again. before he told
his men the Lord had turned His face away?

And how many times does the lonely heart
have to break before it can stop singing?

BLUES

pl. noun

1. Feelings of melancholy, sadness, or depression.
2. A melancholic style of music, typically centering on a twelve-bar sequence based around a standard harmonic progression, and having any of a number of distinguishing characteristics intended to express the performer's melancholy, such as the use of blue notes; a vocal style featuring rasping, growling. or the bending or sliding of notes; and certain recurring lyrical themes and structures.

THE JUKE JOINT PRAYER

Give me some of that old-
soul blues, that back alley
juke joint shoe-slapping blues.
Give me a good woman. Give
me a dance floor. Give me that
open-shirted, high-waisted,
pinstriped blues. Give me sweat.
Give me gin. Give me a rain
that washes me down. Give me
the full-body blues that my grand-
daddies knew. Give me the holy
word and the bourgeois blues.
And give me a river of forgetting,
Lord, at least give me this.

TROUBLE SO HARD

When I say that he ran down that dirt road harder than a light-
ning bolt beats on an oak tree,
I mean his legs were doing work. I mean that his feet blistered
and bled hard, that his head
was beading sweat. I mean we're all trying to get out of these
blues alive before something
catches up.

When I say the police were running after him, I mean they just
wanted to see a black man run
until his legs gave out. I mean they had nothing on him. I mean
that's the way things work:
we're all doomed with the same blues, but I mean some of us
just know better.

When I say he ran faster than the police could muster, I mean
he was shedding everything
that slowed him down. I mean he was running for his life. I
mean that he wanted it more
than they did.

When I say he was running for his family, I mean he had more to
lose. I mean that everything
weighed on him hot and heavy. I mean that he didn't know
where he was running to, only
that he had to run. I mean he was running to me.

When I say the police caught up with him, I mean everyone
gets wise one day. I mean
sometimes luck runs out. I mean they gunned him down like
a dog.

ROBERT JOHNSON
BEFORE THE DEAL

Robert sits by an open window
waiting for nightfall, his steel-string
a breath waiting to be exhaled. The rain outside,
like a bluesman's arpeggio, taps against
the tin roof, finding the holes
and nestling there. It has been two days
since the word came down, two days since sleep.

In the corner, the radio pours out
its oblations to heartache the way a wound
relieves itself of blood. Meanwhile
the clock stirs in short fits, burdened with time.

Say it plain: sometimes the blues takes
and sometimes it gives back.

ARS POETICA

a good blues
doesn't sing
it breathes
it doesn't want
it makes &
it doesn't end
but keeps
bleeding through
a good blues
resonates
a siren
in the harbor
a blackbird
in the morning
it doesn't ask
for anything
it makes plain
even if
the last word
shakes

JAZZ

noun

A type of popular music originating (esp. in ragtime and blues) among African Americans in the southern United States, typically performed by ensembles and broadly characterized by regular forceful rhythms, syncopated phrasing, modifications to traditional instrumental tone and pitch (such as the use of blue notes), and improvisatory soloing.

JAZZ HYMNAL

blessed is the night
     its cool breath, its wild & unyielding music
blessed is the night
     with its horns & teeth, its blindness, its hollering
blessed is the bassline
     that pulsing blue vein that uncoils itself over & over, swelling
blessed is the strain of the piano key
     how it buckles & then lifts again as though hungry
blessed are those who hunger for jazz clubs
     who thirst for their primal dark, two-step on their floorboards
blessed are the half-crazed & dancing
     for their bodies will dive & stumble in oblivion
blessed is the songstress orbiting the microphone
     may hers be the voice that claws through the perpetual
smoke
blessed is the smoke, yes, but blessed is the night
     hasn't it always been a kingdom for the untamed spirit, for the
new?

SATCHMO REFLECTS

After Tyehimba Jess

when the old scats no longer breathe new orleans:

how to shimmy the tongue free of its silken smooth?

how to bury the whitewashed bones without losing muscle?

how to shuck the suit clean off a shivering body?

what bouillon will boil in his veins?

how to dam the cornet at its open mouth?

how to heal the divided soul before it shatters?

what new jive will inhabit the space where teeth once lay?

how to bleed a man of his jazz and then replenish him?

ELLA ON MUSIC

all these years i've stayed close
to music   it wasn't easy
to settle for my second love
dancing was in my snake hips long before
song burrowed in my throat
but i needed more than a bop could offer
needed scat's jagged cadence to lift
my voice from its shallow bed

music lives inside me   bray
of a trumpet   piano-lilt
as long as i stand on these legs
i will raise myself to a band's crescendo
head heavy   tongue lithe with jazz

BEBOP MANIFESTO

we love the sound
a body makes
when it gives itself
to abandon. we
 ove lawless harmony.
we love a song
that burns and
the song that's born
from its ashes.
we love honey-cool
saxophones, tangled
syncopation. we
love the scat after
the scatter. we love
I ke water—all fullness
and weight. we love
heartache. we love
muttering our verses
as though through
broken teeth. we
love when we
want to, die when
we have to. we
love the night
and it loves us
back. we love back.
we love back.

RHYTHM AND BLUES
(ABBR.: R & B)

noun

Any of various kinds of popular music originally (and principally) associated with African-American performers, esp. a style prominent during the late 1940s and 1950s derived from or influenced by the blues and jazz, typically having a strong rhythm and featuring a horn section.

RACE MUSIC

Our business is making music
white enough to cover
even the deepest blues.
We steal to earn our keep.

We pull up troublesome roots
& reconstitute meaning
from a song's skeletal frame.
This is how music becomes echo:

What we don't gut, we bury.
What we don't bury, we bleach
then iron, shred then darn, until
the song no longer knows itself.

BIG MAMA SPEAKS OF ELVIS

If death shows up as a man
in blue denim, says *I want* in a voice
just above a warble, takes
and takes from you, fits your livelihood
in his shirt pocket
then reaches for his comb—
ain't nothing but a shakedown,
a wolf at the door.

I ask you: What's justice?
Is it the cart by itself or the horse
that comes before?

No matter now. Another stone sinks
to the bottom of the river,
another white man
drinks me till I'm dry.
How long, this life.

CREATION MYTH

Bo Diddley, Who Gave Rock His Beat, Dies at 79
—Headline from the New York Times

i.
my body was hungry.
inside me was a rhythm
i couldn't call
a heartbeat. it started in my hips—
the spirit shaking its fists—
then moved up through me,
made me heavy.

ii.
like the world coming
out of the darkness, like
the spirit moving across the water,
a rhythm was born
within me, then scattered without.
i was all hips & foot-stomping,
father to the beat
some called a bedrock.

iii.
all things begin
& end in darkness: my body,
the hollow of my guitar.
once, i played it
like the hammer it was,
but even as i pounded my beat
into its strings, i knew
something would ripple.

iv.
they say every beginning
is lost to time:
mine was a guitar
first touched
by the spirit, then by me,
music the stitch
that joined us.

REVERSE HOMICIDE

For Sam Cooke, after Matt Rasmussen

The girl who goes to call the cops
eats her words, restores the phone

to its hook without mentioning the death.
With shaking hands, the motel staff

return the stolen clothes to their owner
and dress him as they would

a cold china doll. The bones in the dead
man's hands reform. His nose unmangles

itself. Every fist retreats to its rightful
pocket after the dead man is dragged

back to the manager's office,
wiping the trail of blood from the floor.

The broomstick is put back in its closet,
where it lies dormant as its need

is revoked. The dead man rises
when his heart pumps the bullet back

into its gun. And when the manager falls
back into her chair, she watches him

run backwards up the staircase, and
waits to hear a voice that never comes.

SOUL MUSIC

noun

In early use: any of various types of jazz, blues, or gospel music popularized by African Americans; (later spec.) a kind of pop music originating in the Motown sound and incorporating elements of rock music with rhythm and blues.

INTERVIEW WITH BERRY GORDY

Lord knows, we did
                    what we could to keep
the jivers jiving,
                    to move their hips
at pulse's tempo.
                    We did the footwork,
wore the suits &
                    the sequins. We teased
the wigs. We worked
                    the ballrooms & the TV
lounges, the total
                    area of the circuit.
But slick as an oil
                    spill, halfway
between warble
                    & holler, orchestra
& bassline, it was our sound
                    that brought crowds
to the dance floor
                    & took us beyond
the city's narrow
                    limits. For years
our sound was the house
                    we lived in: strong
enough to withstand
                    its own fire &
bold enough
                    to start one. Listen
to what I'm saying:
                    No, our bodies
never knew rest
                    or relief, but we knew
the songs and how
                    to sing them—with bike
chain, saxophone, hand
                    on callused hand.

DAVID RUFFIN LEAVES THE TEMPTATIONS

After Craig Arnold

there was a sound & it was fire   was
harmony & the rasp of a man tethered
to his own hunger   there was hunger
& it was beautiful   there was anguish but
it was called music   every night
there was a stage & on it there was dancing
& a chorus of magpies singing their wordless
& immaculate caw   there was a shuffle
then a measured kick five voices &
a crescendo   a man & his public   some-
times there was a bottle & it was called
passion   sometimes there was anger
& it was gasoline   there was a thought
& in it was separation   still   sometimes
there was a man   he was burning

MARVIN GAYE MOURNS TAMMI TERRELL

you live with soul
because words no longer
speak your grief. two months
since her death, and

the old reliefs have turned raw:
music, now the bell you can't
unring; love, now a wound
bleeding through its suture.

trouble man, if your blues
could sing themselves,
every song would be a siren
calling you to the rocks,

even the clean blue beginning
of the song caught in your throat.

THEY CALL ME NINA

they call me nina. i have sacrificed
my whole life for this name. in the back
rooms of the piano bars, they call me
a work horse—strong, but sometimes
willful. i'm no horse, but i'd be a killer
if i could. in tryon, they called me eunice.
it means *good victory*, a yoke too wide
for my shoulders to bear alone. so i
married young. i'm still not over it. nina,
they call me now. it means *little girl*,
as though i'd never known pain. believe
me, i have sacrificed my whole life
to sing my people's pain. on the street
corners, in the church bathrooms, they
use hoses and firebombs on us. i'm no dog,
but i'd bite back if i could. sometimes
i don't know how i'm still standing. i say
call me nina, but i know they fear negro.
it means *black*, a shade too dark to be
anything but beautiful. i must be beautiful.
when i sing, i sing to uplift. my people,
they've known heartache. in the backstage
lounges, in the silent halls, they say i'm
dangerous. believe me, i'll never be over it.

OTHER C&R PRESS TITLES 2016-2017

NOVEL
That Man in Our Lives by Xu Xi
Spectrum by Martin Ott
A History of the Cat In Nine Chapters or Less by Anis Shivani

SHORT FICTION
The Protester Has Been Released by Janet Sarbanes
Medittions on the Mother Tongue by An Tran

ESSAY
Immigration Essays by Sybil Baker
Je Suis L'Autre: Essays and Interrogations by Kristina Marie Darling

POETRY
Free Boat by John Reed
The Couple Who Fell to Earth by Michelle Bitting
Tall as You are Tall Between Them by Annie Christain
Les Fauves by Narabara Crooker
Imagine Not Drowning by Kelli Allen

ANTHOLOGY
Aliens, Cyborgs, Zombies and the Ongoing Apocalypse:
Sci-Fi Poems of the 21st Century and Beyond
by Travis Denton & Katie Chaple